Scribbles

Songs of the Heart

RAJANI RAJA

WestBow Press books may be ordered through booksellers or by contacting:

WestBow Press
A Division of Thomas Nelson & Zondervan
1663 Liberty Drive
Bloomington, IN 47403
www.westbowpress.com
844-714-3454

ISBN: 978-1-6642-4823-6 (sc)
ISBN: 978-1-6642-4824-3 (e)

Library of Congress Control Number: 2021921813

Print information available on the last page.

WestBow Press rev. date: 12/31/2021

WESTBOW
P R E S S®
A DIVISION OF THOMAS NELSON
& ZONDERVAN

(NIV) Romans 12:6 "We have different gifts, according to the grace given to each of us"

Thanking my God for the creative inspiration.
Dedicating this work to the indescribable Heavenly Father,
my wonderful earthly parents – Raja and Annu,
and my amazing siblings – Aruna and Prakash.
Thank you for your support and letting me be me.

Introduction

Our lives, our dreams
Will remind of us
As the days go by
And soon we will be gone too
But what our dreams created
Will live on to tell our story

These Scribbles, my poems are my thought, my hopes, my dreams, my
questions, my prayer. A fragrant potpourri of all my emotions
All that my heart has to say. The songs from my heart.
This could be you, your story, your song too.

Let's Talk Poetry

Onerous Moi

The craniums deep crevices
Saw the precipitous rise of madness
The endemic right of the dreamer
Lost in the minutiae of her dreams

Like a poète maudit
Gets a serotonin kick from it
But is like vōx clāmantis in dēsertō
Anthropomorphic deus
Hellenistic elysian
But forced by the worldly lycèe

Acting now like a heretic
Notwithstanding my volition given by the constitution
I have become an eponymous rebel
This rapid capitulation
Left an inedible mark
Not on the society but on my soul

Intuition of a mental contagion
And a farce mind
Passed a dictum, a perfect alibi
For the epistemic arrogance

A pyrrhic victory costing my soul
I became a flâneur
To learn the ways of the world
Alas, the prevarications of my mind

Became a sycophant to the world
A pander to them

Forming a consilient story
A bard or troubadour
Knitting stories with iniquity and fidelity

For Your Tomorrow

Burning with rage
Angry at the injustice
Desperate for a change

I fought
Fought to live

Live in a better world

Fought till I lost myself
Sacrificed my today
For a better tomorrow

Dreaming of a tomorrow
A better tomorrow

But will tomorrow remember
My sacrifices
Will it understand my fight?

Will it enjoy what I fought for
Or will it have new, battles to fight

Was my sacrifice in vain
(Not for me
I did enjoy its results in my lifetime)

Will tomorrow know my struggles, my past, my story
Will it fight to preserve it's future? [1]

---

[1] Inspired by John Maxwell Edmonds words "When you go home, tell them of us and say, 'For your tomorrows these gave their today." Enshrined on the Kohima war memorial in Nagaland (India), built to commemorate soldiers who laid down their lives in 1944 during World War-II.

Sentinels of Faith

I am standing there
Waiting for you, for all

Braving sun and storm
Pestilence and mundane

The thousands that breathed into me
Their breath of life
Their hearts touched mine
I can still feel the touch
Of support or just

Everyone is gone
But I am still there
I am standing there
Waiting for you, for all

A refuge from the sun and rain
A refuge for the burdened soul
Or just a praising flower

I have none of it now
None

But I will still be there
Waiting for you, for all

Hoping to see you, one day

Until the earth ravages me
Or the men tear me down
I will be standing there

A sentinel of faith
Sole and Strong
Waiting for you, for all

Mortar and brick
Set on foundation by
Men gone long past

I stand

I stand still but strong
Rock I am but my soul breathes
Temple of God I am
My deity resides in me[2]

[2] This poem is inspired by the church of St.John's Parramatta, my church in Sydney, Australia. Which due to Covid-19 pandemic is closed and members are unable to congregate.

Good Night

Go on, I let you sleep
Not for the weary body
But for the dreamy soul
It yearns to build its castle
With the bricks of memories
And mortar of love

Go on, I wish you good night
Not for the weary body
It's not tired yet
But for the dreamy soul
It wishes to build more of these castles
Where it could hide from the travails of life

She fluttered through the door
At the voice of the choir
She sat there motionless

Immersed in the melody of music

Distracted, I looked at her
She might move to the rhythm of music, dance

But she lay still
Lost, mesmerized

The people around
Who looked at her?
Who walked past her?
Who crushed her under their feet?

She lay there, still, in pieces, the dry fallen leaf
Still
Immersed in the melody of music.

The Inconspicuous Leaf [3]

---

[3] (The title of the poem is to lead you to picture what you are about to read. For some of my poems I like to keep the suspense, so I have the title at the end)

Clouds in the sky

We lost our way
Looking up, at the
Clouds in the sky

We were no explorers
Looking at the stars or clouds
To find our way

We were out to lose our way
To spend more time on the road to nowhere
Our friends and me were in no hurry
To find our way

Back to the world
Where to lose our way
Was foolishness
To walk the untrodden path
With no crooked or curved trail
Nothing to learn or experience
No adventures, no surprises
Was the best way

The ways of the world
Was not to lose your way
Looking up, at the
Clouds in the sky

Is it real?

Oscillating between the real and surreal
We travel where we don't want to go
Leaving behind the real,
In search of what is not real

Being happy in our transient state
To get it all
Forgetting what lies ahead
Which really is real

Questions?

Hope they say
Was this the question
Nay, this is the answer to our question
Question of future, of disappointments, of life…

Some questions are not to be asked
For we know within our heart
The answer

Faith they say
Was this the question
Nay, the answer

Love they say
Was this the question
Nay, the answer
Question of hatred, of pride, of greed…

Before I vanish..

The face veiled by a mask
Colorful and lively
Hid the tears beneath
The world saw the colors
The heart its tears
The aching heart cried
The mind quieted it
Not now, you should be
Standing strong
Strong like a rock
But the rock was crushed to pieces
Its pebbles, some tossed in puddle, in grime
Some found its resting place deep underwater
Some in a lush garden
A few were broken more, crushed, low
To be seen no more

14

Pain Of Awareness

To not know was to not see the dark
And walk as if in light
To know was to see the dark
And still walk in dark

What would have been better?
To know or not to know

To not know was to see the ugly,
But see it beautiful
To know was to see the ugly,
And feel its ugliness

What would have been better?
To know or not to know

Being aware of the pain, unable to heal
Being aware of the joy, unable to enjoy

We live our lives in this pain of awareness

To not know was to miss the love of the loved ones
To know was to see the love but unable to receive it

What would have been better
To know or not to know

We live our lives in this pain of awareness

So why don't we
Feel and cherish every moment
In its full awareness

To be able to do so, is when the
Pain of awareness would be no more
Joy despite the pain, of being aware

The Afternoon Rain

Hot and humid, bellowing flames from the furnace
it's been like this for quite some time
the unrelenting summer was not to exit gracefully
and let the monsoon enter
it was holding its last post

but today the rain was determined
to drench the earth, to soak its beings
it has long been held by the sun
but now can no longer be subdued
it had to let go

pouring out to its heart's desire
which was taken with full arms
by one and all

the parched earth, the dry crops, the thirsty animals
farmers waiting for the showers to feed the crops
earth was waiting to soothe it scorched land
birds and animals were waiting to quench its thirst
everyone had a reason in this season

no one would have got such a great welcome on earth
everyone eagerly awaited its return
so, at last it was here on this afternoon
enveloping everything in its embrace

Oblivious to all the excitement around me,
I was just happy to hear the raindrops, see it
wet the earth
Small streams forming taking along with it the
dirt of the earth
Watch people under their umbrella's trying to
avoid rain
The splash of rain all around, the cool breeze
and the thunder

I sat with my friends, a hot cup of tea and
talks of what all we could do in rain
Reminiscing our childhood days, of playing in
the rain
But now all that seemed immature, obviously
we had grown up
Lost in our world admiring the world around,
until it was time
Time to get back to work

We were back to work, but that afternoon rain
continued
Continued until night, like it had an obligation
To embrace the earth, to drizzle, to drown,
The earth

*Life in the WORD**

(ESV – John 1: 14 "And the Word became flesh and dwelt among us, and we have seen his glory, glory as of the only Son from the Father, full of grace and truth.")

Color

Don't color me
White, black, brown, yellow
No
Maybe on the outside
But it's the same red inside
No
Don't

I will not plead
No
I will not
To look me equal
For you know
Deep inside we are same

God said "Let us make man in our image, after our likeness "[4]

---

[4] (ESV) - Genesis 1:27 "So God created man in his own image, in the image of God he created him; male and female he created them."

Prayers

- *Wounded and bleeding*
I want to give up
But I can't give up, I can't give up on God
It hurts to go on
It hurts even bad to go on without you, God

So little faith, so much doubt
It just hurts to go on
It hurts to give-up

Trials they say are steppingstone
But feel like stumbling blocks
I fall and don't want to get up
Don't even try to get up

It just too much effort to get up
It just easier to give up
To lay in loss and lost

I want to give up
But I can't give up, I can't give up on God
Because I know he will never give up on me

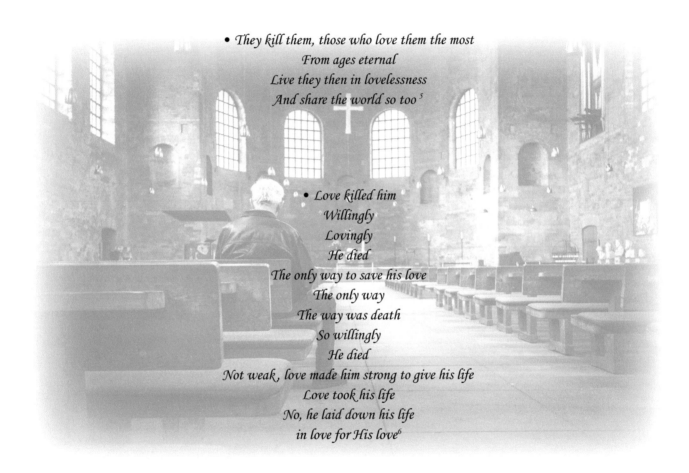

- They kill them, those who love them the most
From ages eternal
Live they then in lovelessness
And share the world so too [5]

- Love killed him
Willingly
Lovingly
He died
The only way to save his love
The only way
The way was death
So willingly
He died
Not weak, love made him strong to give his life
Love took his life
No, he laid down his life
in love for His love[6]

---

[5] (NIV) John 18: 40 - They shouted back, "No, not him! Give us Barabbas!" Now Barabbas had taken part in an uprising.

[6] (ESV) Romans 5: 7 For one will scarcely die for a righteous person—though perhaps for a good person one would dare even to die. 8 but God shows his love for us in that while we were still sinners, Christ died for us.

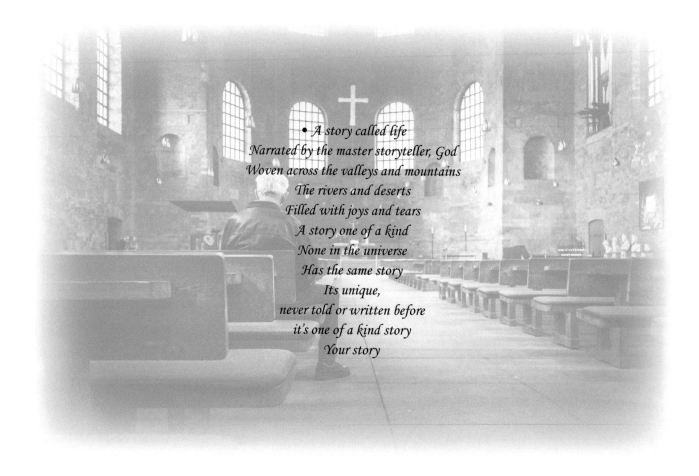

- *A story called life*
Narrated by the master storyteller, God
Woven across the valleys and mountains
The rivers and deserts
Filled with joys and tears
A story one of a kind
None in the universe
Has the same story
Its unique,
never told or written before
it's one of a kind story
Your story

Good Night Lord

I kneel, to pray
To say good night

For helping me through
Another day of my life

I made it through, Thank you, God,
One more plea, as I sleep keep me safe
To rise to another day of your blessing

Before I go, want to ask you how was your day?
Was it full of people asking for blessing just like me? Or were they thanking you for your blessings
Or was it heartbreaking to know that they don't know you after all you have done.
Or living as they want, knowing you
How was your day, God?

Were you tired? Did u get to rest?
Were you happy or sad?
Were you disappointed in me?
Did u ever feel you can't keep going on?
Did u ever want to give up on me, on us

יֵשׁוּעָה

(Pronounced Yeshua, Hebrew for Jesus)

The pain, your suffering
The sadness, your poverty

So much for love
Love it was that hurt you
Love it was that took your life
Yet you love, still loved
And kept loving
Why, why?
Because
that's who I am
Who are you?
I AM, who I AM[7]

---

[7] (ESV) Exodus 3:14 – God said to Moses, I AM, who I Am. And he said, "Say this to the people of Israel, I AM has sent me to you"
(ESV) 1 John 4:8 - Anyone who does not love does not know God, because God is love.

Love

Only the Sun gives free sunlight
Everything else costs
Nothing is free
Not even love
Guess you are free to love anyone or some one

Or maybe not

I know of a ~~Sun~~ Son
Who died for love, freely [8]

---

[8] (NIV) John 3:16 - For God so loved the world that he gave his one and only Son, that whoever believes in him shall not perish but have eternal life.

So, who is it?

Did I think of this?
Did I know this would happen?

Life goes on, I look back
Everything so well planned
The meetings, the escapes
The opportunities found,
The ones missed

Like pieces of a jigsaw puzzle
Put together
To make a beautiful picture
Could it be co-incidence?
Na don't tell me that
It's way too many instances

There is somebody placing the pieces
Arranging them in perfect order
There should be some one
There has to be
Isn't it?

I was building the bridge to the hearts
You broke the cords
I levelled the ground of the rough emotions
You placed boulders there

hoped to build
To dream, to create

I fear one day I might not
Be able to go on
Would sit back in pain
Of the broken world

But then I think
If not me who would?

I cannot sit back, I cannot weaken

What would I answer,
The creator
When questioned, what did I do to its creation

Would I fumble and fall?
Plead ignorance
Or defend myself?

"You had everything I created
You had intelligence, creativity, compassion, love
What did you lack?
What more did you want,
That you ravaged my creation
Damaged beyond repair"

Would I lament, regret my transgress

Hoping for the creator to make one more of the same,
like Earth

That I would cherish and preserve
Or
I would have one more to play with and break
More to destruct and destroy...

What will I do?

29

जिन्दगी

(pronounced Zin-da-gi, in Hindi meaning Life)

आँखें

कुछ ना कह के भी,
सब कुछ कह दिया,
इन आँखों ने सारा राज़ खोल दिया,
जिस ज़ख्म को छुपाते थे अब तक,
उस दर्द का फ़साना बयां हो गया

मेरा मिट्टू बोला

मैं बहुत आभारी हूं तुम्हारा,
तुमने मुझे खाने को दाना दिया,
पीने को पानी दिया,

और रहने को ये आलीशान पिंजड़ा दिया,
कैसे भूल पाऊंगा

सुना है जब इंसान कोई कुकर्म करता है
तो उसे भी पिंजरा (क्षमा कारागृह)
में बंद कर दिया जाता है
हां वहां उसका ख्याल रखा जाता है
उसे दाना पानी मिल जाता है

पर मिट्टू - " में तुम्हें प्यार करता हूं ना"

अगर कारागृह के अफसर कैदी से प्यार करें तो क्या वो आजीवन कारागृह में रहना चाहेगा

Insanity

The serenading plains lay ahead
The hustle lay behind

I walk onward
With each step
Letting go my baggage

I stop and stand still
In emptiness
No longing or desire
No pull of the world

I'm adrift in air
So, relieved
Seems like it was ages ago
I had stopped being myself
I was enjoying every moment
Reliving every moment
Of the lost times

I hear a voice calling me
Its faint and sweet
I look across
I look behind
I see a someone, away in a distance
I see a hand reaching out to me

I run towards it
All excited to show
What I had found
I reached towards it
Fumble, lost for words
I was ecstatic
The joy I found
But I looked like a lunatic

The world did not understand
It took my hand
And pulled me back
Rubbishing everything, I said
It pulled me back
Confused and lost
I let go
And went back...

33

Heart, Mind and Soul

The joys and sorrows of this life
Its ups and downs
Are but just a passing phase

Is the soul perturbed by all this?
Does it weigh upon itself?
These are just at the periphery of
The heart and the mind

The mind has its logic
The heart has its feelings
They think, they dream
When, what you think is not right
Or what you dream of does not come true
Are you hurt?

Is the soul perturbed by all this?
Does it weigh upon itself?

The mind looks and thinks
The heart sees and feels

Two different views of the same thing
So, what is right?

Or what is perceived to be right
Will someone speak up?
But who is listening?
Is it the heart or the mind?

Amen

Say a silent prayer for the wearied souls
That walk the ways trodden by ghosts of past

Amidst the cacophony, I add not discord
I sit amid lives milling around
Eyes moving from one person to another
Their visage, their face, their eyes
the story behind the eyes
the stories hid behind the smile by the mind
but the mirror of the heart, the eyes
does reveals it all
the untold story, is thrown open
for to the one who cares to read it

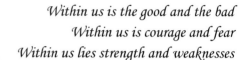

The Hero and The Villain

Within us is the good and the bad
Within us is courage and fear
Within us lies strength and weaknesses

Trying hard to reign in the monster outside
While they breed within
Creeping behind the goodness
waiting for us to lose hope and faith
and become the villain we always feared

Afraid of the demon, the other human
when that is within us

like two sides of a coin, we too have
which side the world sees depends on how it is tossed
would it land heads up, seeing our bright, cheerful side? Our best
or would it land tails up, to see our anger and rage. Our worst

seems like we have no control over it
is it?
or can we?

out there in the solitude high above, can u attain redemption
looks impossible
for the man from the valley below

can we, can I, do it?
How can one sweep away the darkness?

Look up (rise and shine)

Stop
For once
Please

Look up to the life around
Life of flesh and blood
Not to life of pixels and anime

There are smiles waiting to be shared
Tears to be wiped
People to be hugged
Friends to be made (not just friend behind the screen)9

A helping hand to be lent
A friendly shoulder to lean on
A gentle touch, a pat on the back

For once
Please
Look up

The world is waiting for u
On the other side

An afterthought - (Is there a reason
You don't want to look up)

Are u not of this world
You live within the glass screen
Of fantasy and imaginations

---

9 Facebook, Instagram, Twitter friends

My eyes welled up
Tears trickled down my cheeks

At the kindness of the people
Of the people who help the stranger in need
Not tears of sadness
But of pure joy
To see humanity still intact
Though evil may tear through
We will always find the
Thread to sew the spread of life
With love,
With compassion

My eyes welled up
Tears trickled down my cheeks

At the honesty of the finder returning lost belonging
At the selflessness of the soldier who risked his life
Only to die and be forgotten
Not tears of sadness
But of pure joy
To see humanity still intact

Though evil may tear through
We will always find the
Thread to sew the spread of life

With courage
With humility

Stories galore of these
Angels who walk
Amidst the land of desolation
Leaving their trail
For the future to follow

Hope Not Lost

Ερωτήσεις (Pronounced erotíseis meaning Question in Greek)

1. Why is there so much in equality?
Why do some think they are better than others
Why do they insist everyone follow them?
Are they correct, right always?
The wise the foolish
The good the bad

2. Where does one's right to freedom and choice start
Can you decide on behalf of others?

Believe it is done in the best interest of the other
Without knowing what others want?

3. I don't want to fight
I won't fight
(Not because I can't, because I don't want to)
Why do I always have to fight?
Always..
I am tired
Why do I have to fight?
For everything
Everything – I want
I hope of
I dream of
I am worth of…. ??

Love

Would you love me, if I loved you more than Love could ever love.

Love me whole and full
Love my craziness & weirdness
Love my fears & obsessions
Love my freckles and greys
Love me whole and full

I could change for you
But that heart cannot love you
That heart will need in return
Someone
Sane and practical
Fearless and free
Young and strong

Searching

A thousand string that strung
Through my way of life
Made none a music that could last
Some broke off, some didn't sound right

Awaiting that string
With whom I could
play the music of life

A symphony of love
A melody everyone would hum
Till the day goes down

And haunt their dreams until the sun comes up
Oh, I wish to be that string
To meet that string
To be apart, to be different
But sound perfect together
To play together
A song, an ode
To the creator
To his creation – of love, God's love

Alone

Why do you sit alone?
In the rugged path and broken trails
You have no friends
Or you detest companionship
Nay, nary
I sit alone with myself
To experience myself
To be my friend

I have sat with the world for too long
And won their friendship
Which will wane with time
Or die with death
Then I will be all alone, with myself

I sit alone with myself
To know myself
To be my friend

So, at the end of my journey
It will come along
With me to the other end
Never leaving me
Even unto death

Prisoner of Love

Love is to care, care without expecting
That's what true love is

Love is to be free, free to give, free to receive
Perfect love casts out fear [10]

So how can it imprison someone
But it did, or attempted to
To imprison
Imprison the stubborn, the obstinate
Running away
Running towards anger, frustration, rebellion, hatred

The arms of love stopped
Stopped the free man
Ask if he would be a prisoner
Prisoner of love
Be imprisoned in love

Astounded by the absurd suggestion
I am a free man
Free to choose
Free to hate
To rebel

Free to die (To perish in hopelessness)

But you call me
To be a prisoner
A prisoner

Yea, I call you to be a prisoner
A prisoner of love

To be loved
To be cared
To live
To live in hope

He looked amazed, lost…

---

[10] (ESV) 1 John 4:18 - There is no fear in love, but perfect love casts out fear. For fear has to do with punishment, and whoever fears has not been perfected in love.

Still

The radiant sun
The gentle breeze
Caresses my soul
And everything within
I lay bare
My dreamy love soul
Not to be mocked for my frailties
But nourished by nature
Who understands the colors
The tales of love
And the mysteries of heart
Longing to just stay long
Long enough
For my soul to be fed
With food no man can give
Only God through his
Gift of nature
Bestows on us
The gift of peace
And oneness with its creator.

A Wish

A simple wish
I wanted to write
Among the many wishes
Of your friends and love
I did find a blank space
To scribble on

Words to wish you the very best
In everything
Always
Wish all your dreams come true
May happiness walk with you
May love be your companion

But too much good seems
Too good to be true

Broken dreams, missed opportunities, lost friendships, teary eyes
Maybe I should also wish

Because life will be so uneventful
Without a bit of spice and salt
Without a bit of hurt and pain

Miss You

I long to see you
My eyes search for you
The yearning so strong my heart aches

Yearn to feel your face
To feel your touch

But you are far away in a distant land
But not in my heart, you are as near as the air I breathe

My heart always feels your presence
As if you were besides me
My longing so strong
That never was your being
Far from me
 So why do I miss you

Don't say goodbye
It's not time yet
There are stories to tell
There are songs yet to sing

Not yet
Wait
Don't say goodbye

Dreams

कशमकश
(pronounced Kash-ma-kash, refer to a state of mind that's in conflict or dilemma)

Dare to dream
Dare to hope the dreams come true
I dare not
Scared of broken dreams
Scared of taking risks
Scared to love and lose

Living in fear
Scared to be hurt by the brokenness

So do I give up my dreams
Dreams laid up on my heart
Was it just a dream
To be forgotten in sunshine
Or was it to be carried along
Through sunshine and darkness

I don't know
Will never know until I go
To the other side

I want to, will take it, to the
End
Will I go through?
Only time will tell

But until then I will hold on
Hold on with all my might
Strength and mind
With all my heart and love

I will not give up on you
Until you give up on me..

Do I chase my dream?

Do I chase my dream?
Or let it go
Risk losing it all
Just for a dream
A hundred frown for a simple smile

Do I let it pass by?
Without a fight or a struggle
Thinking it's not for me
Do I chase my dream?
Or let it go

Miracles

You will not understand
They say
Dreams don't come true
Miracles don't happen

The kid lifted the butterfly
With broken, battered wings
And helped it fly

The fly in admiration of the confidence of the child
Tried, with all its might
To fly
Not to let down the child
It flew in spite of what it looked
It flew for that one person
Who believed that
Dreams do come true
Miracles do happen

There is another butterfly with broken, tattered wings
Doesn't want to try anymore
Just lay there waiting for
Its end
Said "dreams don't come true
Miracles don't happen now"

Where is that child now, lost
That will help the butterfly with broken, battered wings

The kid trudging along its path
Saw the listless fly, the colorful butterfly
Caressed it
Held it up like trying to say get up, it's
not time yet
Dreams do come true
Miracles do happen

One more of these colorful
Creatures got to fly
And spread it colors
Across the sky

If not for the child and beings with a heart of a child
We would have missed
The flying colors
In this world of black, white, grey

Where is that heart of the child
If we could preserve it for posterity
The word would be colorful
Not just black, white and its shades

If only that child is still alive
Will
Dreams come true and
Miracles will happen

Don't dream for me
मत ख्वाब बूनो मेरै लिये
उमसे पिरोए धागे मेरे नहीं है

Those threads are not of my weave
Nor am I the weaver of these dreams
तो फिर वो ख्वाब मेरे कैसे हुए

It's not their dream
It's mine
It doesn't make them sleep less
It's not their tears
It's mine
How can I make them
Dream my dreams

Dreams

It came alive
At night
When the souls slept
It flew across
Gliding through the mist
Jumping puddles
Cruising through
Whispering hope to the weary passerby
Sneaking up the rouge of night
Scaring the weaklings

Nameless Tales

1. Don't worry,
I'll be fine
It's just a passing phase
The storm will soon ebb
But will leave behind its shreds

2. The storm within
Hidden from all
Awaiting to wreak havoc
Not on humanity
But on self
The sadness deepens

3. Don't expect me to be perfect
I am not
Nor is the world
Why do u want a perfect person in an imperfect world?
Colored plumage in a world which see only black and white

4. Concealed in the interstices
Of my heart
Nuggets of dreams
Veiled by the web of cares
Concealed but not irretrievable
Pretermit but not lost
Hoping one day an adventurous soul
Will choose to cross the trammel of ache and grief
To unearth the treasures of my heart

5. Alone in the crowd
Thirsty by the river
There but not here
Moving but still
Searching far for something near
Within but without
Always looking afar
Missing the joys around
Missing the stranger nearby who could be a friend
Missing the river and looking to drink from a bottle
So much for so little

6. Is it the raindrop?
Or the tears
I wouldn't know
Or maybe I do
But pretend to ignore
And pretend to ignore
Was it me crying alone?
Or the sky crying along with me
Your hurt so unbearable
Couldn't contain it
Her hurt, was it bigger than mine
Or was she crying with me
Who knows?

7.   Shackled by memories
Chained in love
Living in dreams
Rising in hope
In need but contend
Angry but never hating
Inching towards the finish line
But always looking back (hoping to live more)
Hoping against hope
Living despite it all

8.   Some doors close
Some doors open
Sometimes all doors close
And none open

9.   Don't worry, I will not tell
Your secrets to anyone
I don't even tell
My secrets to myself
Keep them hidden in the mind
Because I am sure my heart
Will let it out to my soul

10. Do not say for sure
What you will do tomorrow
For tomorrow has its own plans

Every time I write
I leave a part of me
Impressions of me, soft or hard
On a paper
On a computer

Some will be torn, burned, erased, forgotten
Some gets buried in the depts of the earth
Preserved by the ravages of earth
Some are broken by the creatures under

Will mine last
Only time will tell

Author Biography

Rajani Raja is the poet of the unspoken. Words, sentences, stories, questions, thought, in a common day but never expressed. She carries with her an amazing lens capturing the world around and has a unique knack of weaving them into a symphony of words. Though untrained in poetic language, she has found her own style of writing. Experimenting with words and styles. Reflected in her work is her experiences from widely travelling. At the time of publishing this book, is living in Sydney Australia.

Printed in the United States
by Baker & Taylor Publisher Services